C D C ?

CDC?

William Steig

Farrar Straus Giroux   New York

Library of Congress Control Number: 2002111704
Distributed in Canada by Douglas & McIntyre Ltd.
Color separations by Tien Wah Press
Printed and bound in Singapore by Tien Wah Press
First edition, 1984
New edition, with colored pictures, 2003
1 3 5 7 9 10 8 6 4 2

To Holly McGhee

C U N 10-S-E

U F A 4-N X-N, 9 ?
C, C !

V F E-10 D L-F-N

F-R-E-l E-R S D-P

M-N-U-L S N-C-Q-R

K-C S N N-L-S-S

U R N-2-8-F N Y-S

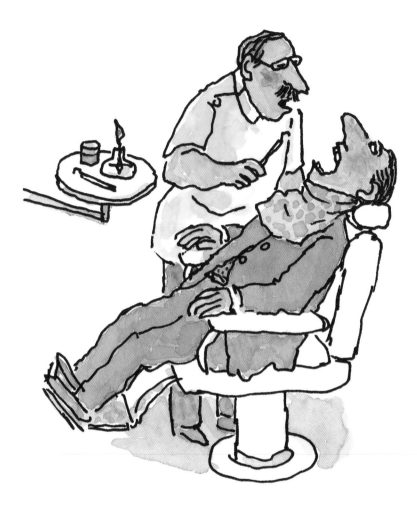

U F D-K N U-R K-9

U F N H ?
I F N L-R-G

I P-T M

I F D Q-R !

U F B-D I-S

E-R I M !

L-X-S N $-S R N A K-F

R T-M S B-N B-1O

I 1-R F U K-R 2 F T

U R N I-D-L Y-F

S A 3-L 2 C U !

U-G-N K-M 2 D C-T

5 N P-N-O

D 1O-R S-N N 2-N

T-D-M

D 2-2 S C-D

S X-U-L-E A 2-P

D 2-M F 2-10-K-M-N

A 2-R F D 4-M

D D-8-T

N-R-E D 8

¢ X-A-V-R

F-N

L

R-A-B-N G-N-E

B-U-T N D B-S

D L-F N D 4-S

N-M-E L-E-N

L-O, R-P

F-E-G

¢-1O-E-L

I-L B U-R-S 4-F-R N F-R

I W !

M I B-N 2 V-M-N ?

F-N U N-E D-¢-C ?

U R E-10 2 X-S !

U R O-D-S !
N U R S-N-9 !

S A D-L !

D ¢-N-L S C-P

I M N-O-¢,
I M A D-¢ U-M B-N

X-I-1O C-N-R-E

D-2-R

S A R-D N-U-L

N-E-1 4 10-S ?
N A Y-L

&-E S A-M-N D R-O

I M I-R N U !

D D-¢ S E-Z-R N D A-¢

A Y-L S

O, C D C !
S X-L-R-8-10 !

D N

A Key to the Wordplay

Page 1   C U N 10-S-E = See you in Tennessee.

Page 2   U F A 4-N X-N, 9 ? = You have a foreign accent, <u>nein</u>?
      C, C ! = <u>Sí, sí!</u>

Page 3   V F E-10 D L-F-N = We have eaten the elephant.

Page 4   F-R-E-1 E-R S D-P = Everyone here is dippy.

Page 5   M-N-U-L S N-C-Q-R = Emmanuel is insecure.

Page 6   K-C S N N-L-S-S = Casey is in analysis.

Page 7   U R N-2-8-F N Y-S = You are intuitive and wise.

Page 8   U F D-K N U-R K-9 = You have decay in your canine.

Page 9   U F N H ? = You have an itch?
      I F N L-R-G = I have an allergy.

Page 10   I P-T M = I pity him.

Page 11   I F D Q-R ! = I have the cure!

Page 12   U F B-D I-S = You have beady eyes.

Page 13   E-R I M ! = Here I am!

Page 14   L-X-S N $-S R N A K-F = Alexis and Dolores are in a cave.

Page 15   R T-M S B-N B-10 = Our team is being beaten.

Page 16   I 1-R F U K-R 2 F T = I wonder if you care to have tea.

Page 17   U R N I-D-L Y-F = You are an ideal wife.

Page 18   S A 3-L 2 C U ! = It's a thrill to see you!

Page 19   U-G-N K-M 2 D C-T = Eugene came to the city.

Page 20   5 N P-N-O = Fife and piano

Page 21   D 10-R S-N N 2-N = The tenor isn't in tune.

Page 22   T-D-M = Tedium

Page 23   D 2-2 S C-D = The tutu is seedy.

Page 24   S X-U-L-E A 2-P = It's actually a toupee.

Page 25   D 2-M F 2-10-K-M-N = The tomb of Tutankhamen

Page 26   A 2-R F D 4-M = A tour of the forum

Page 27   D D-8-T = The deity

Page 28   N-R-E D 8 = Henry the Eighth

Page 29   ¢ X-A-V-R = Saint Xavier

Page 30   F-N = Heaven

Page 31   L = Hell

Page 32   R-A-B-N G-N-E = Arabian genie

Page 33   B-U-T N D B-S = Beauty and the Beast

Page 34   D L-F N D 4-S = The elf in the forest

Page 35   N-M-E L-E-N = Enemy alien

Page 36   L-O, R-P = Hello, harpy.

Page 37   F-E-G = Effigy

Page 38   ¢-10-E-L = Centennial

Page 39   I-L B U-R-S 4-F-R N F-R = I'll be yours forever and ever.

Page 40   I W ! = I double you!

Page 41   M I B-N 2 V-M-N ? = Am I being too vehement?

Page 42   F-N U N-E D-¢-C ? = Haven't you any decency?

Page 43   U R E-10 2 X-S ! = You are eating to excess!

Page 44   U R O-D-S ! = You are odious!
      N U R S-N-9 ! = And you are asinine!

Page 45   S A D-L ! = It's a deal!

Page 46   D ¢-N-L S C-P = The sentinel is sleepy.

Page 47   I M N-O-¢, I M A D-¢ U-M B-N = I am innocent, I am a decent human being.

Page 48   X-I-10 C-N-R-E = Exciting scenery

Page 49   D-2-R = Detour

Page 50   S A R-D N-U-L = It's a hardy annual.

Page 51   N-E-1 4 10-S ? = Anyone for tennis?
      N A Y-L = In a while.

Page 52   &-E S A-M-N D R-O = Andy is aiming the arrow.

Page 53   I M I-R N U ! = I am higher than you!

Page 54   D D-¢ S E-Z-R N D A-¢ = The descent is easier than the ascent.

Page 55   A Y-L S = A wild ass

Page 56   O, C D C ! = Oh, see the sea!
      S X-L-R-8-10 ! = It's exhilarating!

Page 57   D N = The end